HENRYK
WIENIAWSKI

CONCERTO № 1

VIOLIN

ORCHESTRA

F-SHARP MINOR ✦ FIS-MOLL

OPUS 14

MUSIC MINUS ONE

MMO

3187

SUGGESTIONS FOR USING THIS MMO EDITION

WE HAVE TRIED to create a product that will provide you an easy way to learn and perform this concerto with a complete accompaniment in the comfort of your own home. Because it involves a fixed accompaniment performance, there is an inherent lack of flexibility in tempo. The following MMO features and techniques will reduce these inflexibilities and help you maximize the effectiveness of the MMO practice and performance system:

We have observed generally accepted tempi, but some may wish to perform at a different tempo, or to slow down or speed up the accompaniment for practice purposes. This album includes a slower 'practice tempo' version (see note below). However, for even more flexibility, you can purchase from MMO specialized CD players and recorders which allow variable speed while maintaining proper pitch. This is an indispensable tool for the serious musician and you may wish to look into purchasing this useful piece of equipment for full enjoyment of all your MMO editions.

Where the performer begins a piece solo or without an introduction from the accompanying instrument, we have provided a set of subtle taps before the movement as appropriate to help you enter with the proper tempo.

Chapter stops on each CD are conveniently located throughout the piece at the beginnings of practice sections, and are cross-referenced in the score. This should help you quickly find a desired place in the music as you learn the piece.

Chapter stops have also been placed at orchestra entrances (e.g., after cadenzas) so that, with the help of a second person, it is possible to perform a seamless version of the concerto alongside your MMO CD accompaniment. While we have allotted what is generally considered an average amount of time for a cadenza, each performer will have a different interpretation and observe individual tempi. Your personal rendition may preclude a perfect "fit" within the space provided. Therefore, by having a second person press the pause ❚❚ button on your CD player after the start of each cadenza, followed by the next track ▶▶❙button, your CD will be cued to the orchestra's re-entry. When you as soloist are at the end of the cadenza or other solo passage, the second person can press the play ▶ (or pause ❚❚ button) on the CD remote to allow a synchronized orchestra re-entry.

We want to provide you with the most useful practice and performance accompaniments possible. If you have any suggestions for improving the MMO system, please feel free to contact us. You can reach us by e-mail at mmogroup@musicminusone.com.

ABOUT THE 'PRACTICE TEMPO' DISC

AS AN AID during practice, we have included a second compact disc featuring a full-speed version of the complete reference version of the concerto, followed by a second 'practice tempo' version of the accompaniments which have been slowed by approximately 20%. This will allow you to begin at a comfortably reduced speed until technique is more firmly in grasp, at which time the full-speed (or 'traditional' tempo) version can be substituted.

MUSIC MINUS ONE

3187

CONTENTS

LEOPOLD AUER'S NOTES ON THE CONCERTO

*L*EOPOLD *A*UER *(1845-1930), one of the great violin virtuosi of the late 19th and early 20th centuries, described Wieniawski's two violin concerti as "brilliant and written with an eye to virtuoso effect, and...[they] maintain their place as favorite repertoire numbers in concert and recital." In the early 1920s he wrote the following performance suggestions for the First Concerto:*

Wieniawski's Concerto No. 1, in F-sharp minor, op. 14, which the composer wrote while still a young virtuoso, already shows the lion's claws. It is conventional only in form. Otherwise this concerto, especially in its first movement with its heroic Principal Theme in tenths...proves to be the creation of a young iconoclast who seizes every opportunity to reveal his exceptionally brilliant technical powers.

After the passage-work which precedes it, the songful Second Theme in A major [Bar 130]:

makes all the more effective an impression. At [Bar 153] we find a most characteristic passage, formed of a number of sequential chords:

interrupted by scales in thirds and octaves, which offer both the left hand and the right wrist grateful material for perfection exercises. The Cadenza—in spite of the *staccato* and *spiccato* passages which characterize the theme and its development—is conceived in the pathetic style, and should so be played. The full and detailed manner in which the Cadenza (and for that matter the entire concerto) has been provided with expression marks practically precludes any possibility of misunderstanding the composer's wishes and intentions, if the student carefully observes them.

If the Concerto in F-sharp minor does not, perhaps, correspond to the musical ideals of the present day, it is, nevertheless, a noteworthy individual contribution to violin literature and a valuable musical study of the period which followed upon the death of Paganini and of Ernst.

—

The Second Movement, "Preghiera" *(Larghetto),* does not call for extended consideration. It is a "Prayer," very short, and very simply conceived which, in addition to a warm, beautiful tone, demands for its proper interpretation the inward conviction of the believer whose invocation rises to the skies with full sincerity and faith.

—

The Third Movement, "Rondo" *(Allegro giocoso)* has a theme which supplies a welcome exercise in the short, dotted *martelé* stroke. The stroke should come from the wrist; yet if the development of a more powerful tone seems desirable, the student will do well to use the forearm in connection with the wrist. He will be able to judge by the *quality* of the tone he produces how far and to which degree the forearm may be brought into action in order to preserve

intact the tonal beauty of the bowing.

At the *Maggiore* [Bar 79] appears the Second Theme:

which should be played with much warmth; and at [Bar 212] it repeats on the G-string, an octave lower; while later, in the orchestra, it serves as a foundation for the graceful variations of the solo violin. The Coda marked Finale:

quite aside from its melodic content, is an admirable exercise for the short *détaché* and may be played, as preferred, in the middle or at the point of the bow. It might be mentioned, in addition, that the prescribed *ben ritmico* may be secured by an exact marking of the accent on each triplet.

—Leopold Auer

HENRYK WIENIAWSKI

ENRYK WIENIAWSKI was born in Lublin, Poland, on 10 July 1835 to a celebrated family of musicians. His uncle was the well-known pianist Edouard Wolff, and his mother was also an excellent pianist. At a very young age, Henryk began studying violin with Jan Hornziel, and was immediately recognized as a talent to be reckoned with. He was accepted into the Paris Conservatoire at age eight, where he excelled. In 1846 he was awarded First Prize, and began studying with Lambert Massart. A series of concert performances in St. Petersburg followed, and there the young virtuoso came to the attention of Henri Vieuxtemps.

Despite his increasing celebrity, he returned to the Conservatoire and began his composition studies in earnest. Then, in 1851, he began a concert tour in the company of his younger brother, Józef, who was already a successful pianist. By the completion of that tour in 1853, his compositions included the *Souvenir de Moscou; Polonaise No. 1;* and other concert pieces. But it was his Violin Concerto No. 1 in F-sharp minor, op. 14, which put him on the map. This spectacular composition was a tremendous success with its bravura technique, memorable melodies and pure romantic swagger, with a tip of the hat to his idol, Nicolò Paganini.

In 1858 he performed with famed pianist-composer Anton Rubinstein in Paris. Rubinstein convinced Wieniawski to join him in St. Petersburg from 1860 to 1872, and there he exerted a decisive influence on the growth of the Russian violin school. Aside from acting as professor of violin from 1862 to 1868 at the conservatory in St. Petersburg, he became leader of both the orchestra and the string quartet of the Russian Musical Society. During this period he composed much renowned violin music, including the *Etudes-caprices,* op.18, the *Polonaise Brillante,* op. 21, and his most well-known work, the Second Violin Concerto in D minor, op.22 (available on MMO CD 3113). The latter work debuted in St. Petersburg on 27 November 1862, with Anton Rubinstein's famed brother Nikolai conducting.

Wieniawski embarked with Anton Rubinstein on their legendary year-long U.S. tour in 1872, which encompassed over two hundred concerts. Despite the drain of such a schedule, Wieniawski stayed on for a second lucrative year and toured with Paulina Lucca. In 1875 he accepted a two-year professorship at the Brussels Conservatory. In 1876 he also toured Germany during which he engaged in a competition with Pablo de Sarasate. Despite a heart affliction, Wieniawski continued to tour and appeared in London in February and June, and Berlin in November of that year. On 11 November 1878 he had to stop during a performance of his second concerto: the great violinist Josef Joachim, who was in the audience, quickly moved into action and, with Wieniawski's violin in hand, completed the concert with a rendering of Bach's *Chaconne*. At the end of Joachim's performance, Wieniawski, having recovered somewhat, embraced his friend on stage in gratitude.

He continued to tour with great success, though he suffered yet more health-related problems. Also in financial difficulties, his many friends organized a benefit concert in St. Petersburg to raise money for him, his wife and his children. His untimely death on 31 March 1880 in Moscow came two months before the birth of his daughter, Irene.

Wieniawski left a void upon his death. His unique combination of technical wizardry *a la* Paganini, and his ability to conjure heart-rending melody, made him sorely missed by the public and by his peers alike. Fritz Kreisler marveled at his intense use of *vibrato*; Anton Rubinstein dubbed him "the greatest violinist of his time"; and Leopold Auer said that "... since his death no violinist has ever seemed able to recall him."

Aside from his many compositions, his *L'école moderne* and *Etudes-caprices* stand with Paganini's Caprices as the most musical and demanding group of etudes for the violin; and his two violin concerti represent a very special and memorable pair of High Romantic concerted works for the instrument.

MMO 3187

CONCERTO № 1
for
Violin and Orchestra
F-sharp minor 𝄞 Fis-moll
op.14

Henryk Wieniawski
(1835 - 1880)

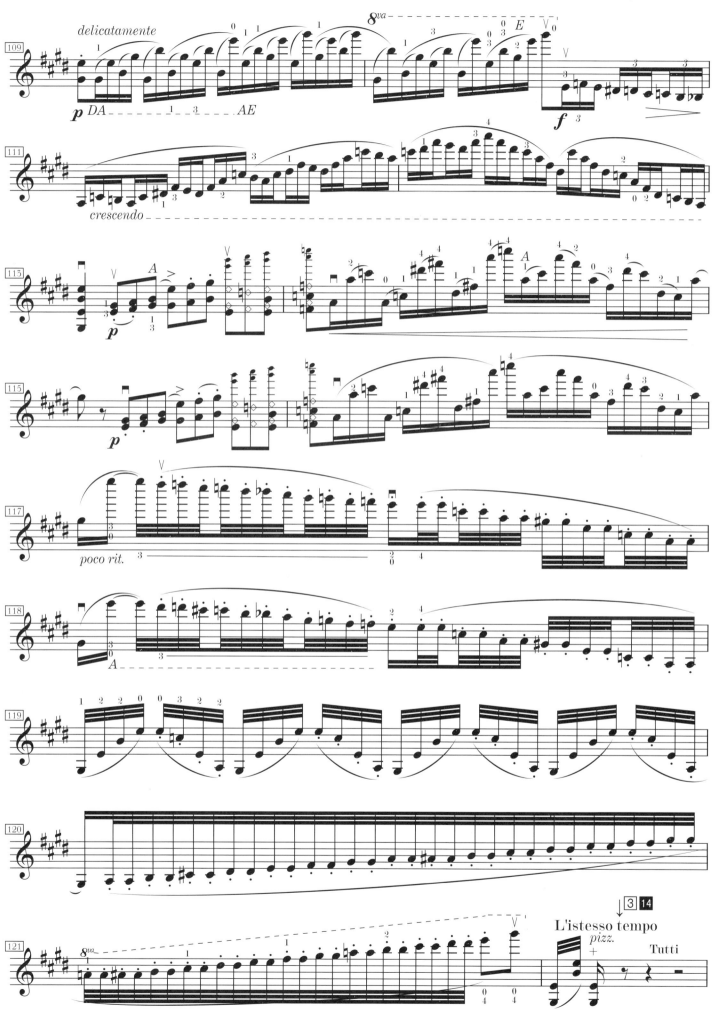

11

MMO 3187

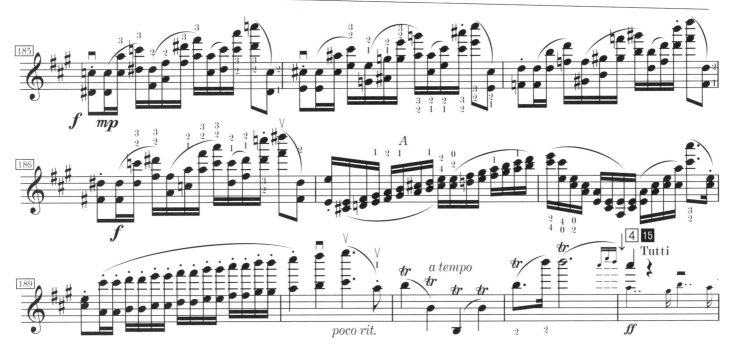

* Originally to the end in f sharp major

II. Preghiera

III. Rondo

Maggiore

MUSIC MINUS ONE
50 Executive Boulevard
Elmsford, New York 10523-1325
800.669.7464 U.S. ← 914.592.1188 International

www.musicminusone.com
mmogroup@musicminusone.com

MMO 3187   Pub. No. 00290   Printed in Canada